The Peaceful Life

Slowing down, choosing happiness, nurturing your feminine self, and finding sanctuary in your home

FIONA FERRIS

ISBN: 9798562633088

Other books by Fiona Ferris

Thirty Chic Days: *Practical inspiration for a beautiful life*

Thirty More Chic Days: *Creating an inspired mindset for a magical life*

Thirty Slim Days: *Create your slender and healthy life in a fun and enjoyable way*

Financially Chic: *Live a luxurious life on a budget, learn to love managing money, and grow your wealth*

How to be Chic in the Winter: *Living slim, happy and stylish during the cold season*

A Chic and Simple Christmas: *Celebrate the holiday season with ease and grace*

The Original 30 Chic Days Blog Series: *Be inspired by the online series that started it all*

30 Chic Days at Home: *Self-care tips for when you have to stay at home, or any other time when life is challenging*

The Chic Author: *Create your dream career and lifestyle, writing and self-publishing non-fiction books*

The Chic Closet*: Inspired ideas to develop your personal style, fall in love with your wardrobe, and bring back the joy in dressing yourself*

Contents

Introduction

Living in a nourishing, loving, orderly environment is important to us all, now more than ever before. It is just easier to function from a calm place, not only physically, but mentally as well. Bringing peace to our everyday life helps us to do what we need to do and enjoy ourselves along the way.

We can't control the outside world, but we can control our inner world – how we think – along with our own external world – where we live, and what and who we surround ourselves with.

It is especially important to have our own place of sanctuary in the world: at home when we are there, and within ourselves when we are out.

The Peaceful Life was written to be a little pocket of calm – a place you can dip into for a soothing read. When you have five minutes, reading a chapter or even a few pages will hopefully feel like you are wrapped up cozily in a big fluffy rug, being comforted and supported.

This book also contains many practical ideas for things you can do to have your life be more peaceful, as well as inspiration to simplify and beautify for a more feminine and restorative way of being. I have included favourite snippets from my blog *How to be Chic*, and some chapters were inspired by posts I have written.

I feel like my role in this world is to share my inspiration with others through my writing. I know how uplifting it feels to read a book and be bursting with ideas afterwards as well as feel indescribably happy for some reason.

It's a fabulous day when you come across a gold nugget in a book which provides you with a new, different, or better way of thinking about something, and I hope you find those nuggets in my books too.

Thank you to reader Victoria S. for suggesting an idea for a book which sparked off *this* book. When she emailed me with her thoughts, I had that exciting 'Yes!' feeling in my stomach, and knew it would be the next book I wrote. Once I started writing, the book veered off in the direction it chose, as books often do, and I couldn't be happier with how it has turned out. I hope you love it too!

With all my best from bright and rainy Hawke's Bay in the southern hemisphere spring,

Part 1:
The Serene Self

FIONA FERRIS

Chapter 1.

What do you stand for?

William Shakespeare said, *'To thine own self be true'*.

It can sometimes be hard to work out how to be true to one's self though, and seem like such a big question that it is easier just to carry on with life as it is. A wonderful thought to ask yourself is, 'What do I stand for?' Pondering this helps usher in thrilling possibilities and new or tweaked directions to steer yourself towards.

When I first heard this question, 'What do I stand for?', it wasn't immediately apparent. I knew the kinds of things I enjoyed doing, but it took some thinking about *what I stood for*. But when I did find out? Well, it opened up a whole new sense of appreciation and contentment for my humble life, which sometimes felt like it was too small and quiet to make any real impact on myself or others. I finally got what I was about and also that it was okay to feel happy and enjoy my life in the quiet and creative way in which I lived it.

And it will be the same for you. Why not ask yourself:

What do I stand for?
What is important to me?
What do I value?
What do I love to think about?

Actually writing down answers to these questions will give you great clarity on how you want to live your life. You will find it easier to identify what adds to your happiness and what takes away from it. You will find simple shifts you can make which greatly enhance your daily expression.

Let me share with you what I came up with, and it may give you some starting points for yourself.

For me, I found that I stand for inspiration, creating and appreciating beauty, and living in a peaceful way. I stand for serenity in outlook, lifestyle, and with food. I believe in each of us making the most of ourselves and treating ourselves to what truly makes us happy in life.

I believe a positive mindset contributes to our wellbeing, and that each of us has the brilliant opportunity to create our own incredible life. We can have our feet on the ground and live in the real world, but we don't need to be *of* the real world. We can be down-to-earth *and* have our head in the stars at the same time.

We can design our lifestyle: our home, wardrobe, and state of mind, to be as pretty and as delicate as we'd like it to be. And, we get to choose what brings us joy! We don't need to go along with anyone else's rules.

My ideal world is rose-tinted, floral-scented, and sparklingly effervescent. I do my daily chores and get things done, and I also immerse myself in my own magical world through my writing, how I keep my home, and what I fill my mind with.

I read books, watch movies and populate my thoughts with beauty and inspiration. My home is simply decorated, but it has pockets of exquisiteness which elevates my frequency.

And none of this takes much money. If you choose to look upon the world as an enchanted place full of possibility and love, it is. You can be aware of what's going on and do what you can, without feeling bogged down by perpetual bad news which you can do nothing about.

And far from being selfish, you will find that you have more to give when you are living in alignment with your values. You will feel happier for no reason and this lightness of being will spill over onto others; with your words, your actions, and your energy.

What do you stand for?

Think about the things you value and see if they translate into how you live your life.

Firstly, dream up all the words and phrases that resonate with you such as my words earlier in this chapter, which are: inspiration, creativity, beauty, serenity, happiness, positivity, head in the stars, feet on the ground, simplicity, exquisiteness, and an elevated frequency. One phrase I didn't mention but that I love, is WOW-factor. Just asking myself how I can bring WOW-factor to a particular area of my life really zings my bell, and turns everything around.

Approach it from the other side too, by listing the parts of your life that you are least satisfied with. Take the opposite of those areas, and see what value they match up with. Perhaps it is your weight. If you are unhappy with your weight, you would value the opposite, which might be health, slimness or fitness, etc. Choose the option that most motivates you.

You have now discovered that, for example, health is a value of yours and something that you would like to stand for. It's incredible but the simple act of claiming 'health' will help you start to make different decisions when shopping for groceries or deciding whether or not to go for a walk that day.

For me, I might know that being healthy is good, but what really lights me up is the thought of looking amazing in my clothes. So, my word might be *fashionista*, which creates a little thrill in my chest

THE PEACEFUL LIFE

and helps me make healthier food choices through the lens of style.

We are all different in how we are motivated, so doing this fun exercise will spotlight bespoke inspiration just for you.

Effortless self-improvement

Another bonus of uncovering what you stand for, is that you will make desired changes in an easy manner.

I value serenity, peace-of-mind and tranquility, but it wasn't until I saw how good those words felt that I could finally let go of being a bit of a drama queen and taking offense easily. I now let things wash over me for the most part, because I don't want to give up my serenity. It's more important to me than proving a point. And the rare times when I do put my foot down, people listen!

I value simplicity, so our home is consistently being decluttered, organized, simplified and tidied. When I get busy or are less motivated and don't do these things as regularly, it feels heavy. When I pursue simplicity by cleaning out and cleaning up, I feel buoyant again.

In these two examples, I found out what I most happily aligned with, and the rest fell into place. It really does feel like you are working with nature and energy and going in the same direction, versus pushing up against something that you want to change.

9

When there is something you are really unhappy about in your life, it can feel like that challenge is an immovable rock. But by approaching things from a different angle, the rock becomes lighter and less heavy, and eventually shatters away like a crystal glass, with pieces floating up into the atmosphere until it has completely disappeared.

Have the courage and faith to love what you love and stand for what you stand for. Don't let anyone else tell you how you should be, think, feel or live. Contemplate what you are most aligned with and make a commitment to yourself that you will go forth with pride in your choices today, and every day.

It will be the making of you.

Your peaceful life tips:

- You can find **lists of personal values** on the internet, so do some online research if you are stuck for a starting point. Choose those that you like, and go from there.

- Think about **what is important to you** and add those things to your list. One example for me is that I love getting good value for money. (Sidenote: I think it's funny that one of my values is value!) But just knowing that stops me feeling bad that I like to hunt down a bargain. I don't go as far as I used to, because, I value serenity as I've said. So I check out options for something I want to buy, but I don't spend weeks on end researching it. When I really need something, I find the best, and best-value, option at the time, buy it and move on with my life.

The cool thing is that you can completely tailor your values list to your own personal preferences. Personalized values – how very elegant!

- If you find yourself triggered by a situation or becoming angry, **see what is setting you off**. Which of your values are being pushed against? Perhaps you see someone being intimidating, and a value of yours is kindness. Add everything you find to your list.

I promise you, seeing this list come together with all these beautiful and positive words will feel so good. **Read them often**. Write a pretty list and keep it in your wallet for when you need some mental refreshment or to calm yourself down when you are feeling het up. Photograph the list and keep it as a screensaver on your phone too.

Your values will boost your spirits as well as keep you on the right track for *you*. Alignment is everything!

Chapter 2.
Cultivating calmness

Someone once commented that I live a very serene life, and I do! I have created a peaceful and calm life for myself *by design*, simply because it is the way I desire to live. I am naturally quite an exuberant person, so cultivating calmness balances me out. I can tip one way or the other, but I always come back to centre. It's lovely there.

There's a lot to be said for living a simple and peaceful life. I guess it all comes down to your personality; some love the drama and fireworks, but for me, the calmer the better. It just feels good.

Peace, order, harmony and wellbeing. These words are like balm to the soul.

It helps to let things wash over you. You don't need to get upset over some small slight or fight someone else's corner. If there is an issue that is nothing to do with you, try and stay out of it.

This is something that has caused me stress in the past, when I inserted myself into a seemingly small matter between two family members. I wasn't asked to be part of it, and neither party needed me to, but I made it my business. I still don't know why I did that, but it caused me mental anguish and taught me a valuable lesson.

Along the same lines, I can't be doing with dramatic relationships. My husband Paul and I are both easy-going Librans and I love that we have a drama-free, non-arguing household. I cannot agree with the advice which says, 'If you don't have arguments there is something wrong'. We both feel awful if there is even 1% tension in the air and must resolve things straight away.

I know my quiet life might sound so boring to someone else, and that reminds me of another thing that helps with my serenity – I care less about what other people think than I used to. It's so freeing. I don't mean that I don't care about people or would intentionally hurt them; it's just that I do what I do, and they get to think what they think.

Consciously simplifying your life helps with serenity too. Keep your home in order, and focus on minimizing possessions in a gentle and slow living kind of way.

I subscribe to very few email lists, regularly prune my internet bookmarks, and decluttering is part of my daily routine. In areas that I use regularly such as the bathroom and kitchen, I am constantly tidying, organizing, and using things up before I buy more. I am not always perfect at this and can still over-buy, but it feels much better when I have just the right amount of products, ingredients or food-stuffs to hand.

Claiming calm for yourself

Cultivating calmness on a daily basis can help you feel joyful and happy most of the time. It nurtures a softness of being when you:

- Remember to be accepting of yourself and others.
- Speak in a smooth and pleasant voice, using a quiet tone.
- Nurture harmonious relationships.
- Are a kind and caring person.
- Feel compassionate towards other people and also animals.
- Get enough rest.
- Spend time by yourself, as much as you need.
- Do things that make you feel happy.
- Have neat and orderly surroundings.
- Infuse gentleness into your being.
- Listen well to others.

This in turn lets you slow down, and helps you appreciate all the simple things in life too.

For me, it is:

- Walking with my dogs in the paddock.
- Writing my books.
- Prepping vegetables and batch cooking meals.
- Lighting candles and incense.
- Playing music every day.
- Appreciating snoozing cats and dogs lying near the cozy fire in the winter, or laying around on the sun-soaked grass in the summer.
- Padding around at home, pottering and organizing things.
- Catching up with friends on the weekend for dinner and wine.

It really does come down to a decision to live in a calm way. Once you have made the choice to lead a simple and tidy life, most of the time you will be heading towards that. When you veer off track you will wonder why you feel out of sorts. That ungrounded feeling is there to remind you why you choose to live the way you do.

The click

You will be at your happiest when you feel like you're in 'the click'. It's hard to explain the click, but you will know when you are there. The click to me is when things are flowing freely, my energy is high yet relaxed, and I feel content and peaceful while being effortlessly productive.

Sometimes I can get into the click without thinking about it, and other times I need to give myself a helping hand. As I come across activities which make me feel amazing afterwards, I write them down on my 'feel good' list. I choose from this list to get back into my wellbeing, and my click.

Things such as:

- Listening to motivational videos and audios.
- Playing around in my wardrobe – tidying it, mending clothes, making a capsule collection or look-book.
- Watching movies where the main character is slim, stylish and confident.
- Doing laundry often: having everything washed, dried and put away.
- Wearing clean, comfortable clothes.
- Decluttering and organizing areas of my home one at a time.
- Meal-prepping ahead of time so I don't arrive in the kitchen hungry with food still to make.
- Letting food and supplies run out as long as possible before I go grocery shopping. Substituting ingredients if necessary.
- Using things up from the fridge, freezer and pantry.

Having an 'emptier' fridge is something I have come to see is enjoyable for me; I feel so relaxed when I open my fridge to see wiped-clean shelves and a tidy assortment of food that is fresh and enticing. When I have too much in my fridge it is crowded and hard to see everything, and food can be wasted if it hides for too long. It's rare that this will happen for me, but the thought keeps me ever vigilant!

We all need to find out what gives us the most happiness, and I think this simple and slow lifestyle is a big one for me (maybe you too?)

Fixing a bad day

If you ever find yourself out of sorts and want to feel more peaceful and grounded, ask yourself, 'What can I do to bring a sense of peace to my day?' You will usually come up with a few ideas and they really can help, no matter how small. These thoughts can help you feel peaceful and content, and your day will go better.

As well, focus on peace as a feeling and you can actually feel it settle on you. Saying to yourself, 'I want to feel peaceful', helps to do just that. Then, depending on where you are, you could take the following actions.

- **Get yourself organized**. A sense of order helps you feel calmer. It might be your work desk, your living room, bedroom or kitchen. No need to tidy the entire house or workspace, just spend five minutes where you are.

- **Change into cozy clothing** and spray on a comforting perfume if you are at home. If you are out or at work, washing your hands and putting on handcream, as well as freshening up your makeup and tidying your hair (a quick few minutes in total), can help you feel reset and ready to finish that job. Doing this clears your head.

- Make sure you have **yummy, gourmet meal provisions**. Choose something natural and elegant, such as a crisp apple and a few slices of cheese. Or my favourite at-home lunch of two scrambled eggs with something fresh such as a sliced tomato. Your physical body prefers this over a snacky bag of fake stuff (something I have to remind myself of often).

- **Play uplifting music** – perhaps a sexy French Buddha Bar/ Hôtel Costes mix, Emma Shapplin, classical violin, or whatever brings about a sense of contentment for you.

All these little things add up and before you know it you will feel great again. Plus, remind yourself that 'tomorrow will be a better day', because it always is, isn't it?

Your peaceful life tips:

- Find out what helps you **feel aligned with happiness** and to get into 'the click' and do more of those things. Start your own feel good list like mine, where you write down things you do that bring about a peaceful and lovely feeling afterwards.

- Stockpile ideas which you know will help you **get back on track** with your wellbeing if you find yourself out of kilter, and use them when necessary.

- Think about the ***flavour* of life that you want to live**. If it is a life of calm and ease, like me, work out how you can make that happen. Put little changes into place and relax your state of being. You can decide to be that person now.

- Don't let anyone put you down for what you desire. You don't need to justify your choices to anybody; **the only person who needs to be happy with them is you**. (Within reason of course, and I know we all have to live with, and get along with, other people, but I'm sure you get what I mean!)

You might decide, for example, not to flare up when someone teases you. The outcome is that the teasing will likely stop because they have nowhere to go after that. Even better, play along with them – agree with them. It will deflect tension in an instant, maybe even promote laughter amongst everyone, and peace is restored.

Chapter 3.

The magic of happylists

Like me, you might love the thought of journaling and of being a person who journals regularly, but the reality can be less like that. The actual word 'journaling' sometimes seems a bit heavy, don't you think? You feel like you have to follow a journal checklist, commit to journaling every single day or what's the point, work out horrible feelings, get a special pre-printed book to fill out... so much pressure!

What I often do instead is indulge in a happylist. Happylists are short and sweet, take no time at all, do not judge you if you haven't done one for a while, and are completely adaptable to whatever you feel like doing when you open your notebook.

Some people might write them on their phone or tablet, or on the computer. I do tons of inspirational writing on my computer, but for my happylists I like to have a small, special notebook that travels around the house with me.

It goes between my office and my bedroom mostly, but I find that I usually use it in my bedroom, either before bed or in the morning. I work from home now, but if I went to work each day, I'd probably tuck it into my bag, because not only is this notebook fun to write, it can be lovely to read back too if you have a spare moment and feel like filling your head with pretty coloured balloons of happiness. It truly can lift your vibration in just a few minutes.

How to 'do' happylists

There are loads of different categories, and once you start creating your own happylists, you will find that you can't help discovering new ones all the time. In their purest form, happylists are precious little bundles of inspiration which just happen to come in many different flavours.

Here are styles I have used so far, to help you start off your happylist collection:

- 10 ideas to try, mostly concentrated on a particular topic.
- Listing down all the good things in your life a.k.a. a gratitude list.
- Things you are excited about right now – new ideas and happy thoughts that are top of mind.

- Fresh and new ideas you want to try out.
- Today's thoughts that are percolating around.
- A new daily schedule to try.
- Your current life-goals.
- Brainstorming a list of ideas on a particular topic that has taken your fancy.
- An actual happylist of things that are making you happy right now.
- Channeling inspiration from a person, decade or idea (i.e. 90s style, Coco Chanel).
- How you are so happy and lucky (more gratitude).
- Exciting goals and ideas in one area of your life.
- Thoughts that delight you and make you feel light and euphoric.
- Things you like doing (to do more of).
- Things you don't like doing (to minimize if possible, or find out ways to make them more enjoyable).

Why use a small notebook?

I recommend using a small notebook (the long, skinny ones are especially good, as are notebooks that are similar in page size to a Kindle screen) simply because they provide a nice, finite end to your writing for that session.

On a larger-paged journal you might think, 'I'll count ten ideas, or write down ten things I'm excited about today.' But then you have to count ten lines, and the page might be two-thirds full which means you have to start a new list part-way down and carry it over to the next page. These things bother me! So with a small notebook, you aim to fill in one page. It's nice and easy. You might not end up with *exactly* ten ideas, but you will always come away with a page full of goodness.

It's a great idea to date the top of each page and put your 'topic' next to the date as well.

Some of my examples to start you off

I am always nosy about other people's inspiration and what they write about, so I want to share some of mine with you, to spark off new ideas and motivation for *your* happylist notebook pages.

~~

Things I like:

- Driving places locally, by myself
- Sunny weather when I'm at home
- Writing my books
- Chopping vegetables for a dinner recipe
- Reading on my Kindle
- Pretty colours in my line of sight
- Stretching my body, lying down on the floor
- Having a massage
- Journaling (in my own way, of course!)

- Having a tidy home
- Decluttering and donating
- Decluttering and selling things at the auction house

~~

As you can see it's not a ground-breaking list, but remembering all the little things I enjoy really does put me in a good mood. This in turn helps me feel positive about the future, and reminds of all the small things that I can do at any time.

And another couple:

~~

Happylist

- Feeling good about decluttering and being minimal
- Having admin, paperwork and financials up-to-date
- A clear kitchen counter and spacious fridge
- Using things up in the kitchen and bathroom
- How I feel when I am pottering and organizing
- Having spa time after dinner with a face mask and moisturizer
- Writing a new book, getting excited by all my ideas

- Cooking new recipes

~~

Exciting Ideas

- Doing a one-day retreat at home: research retreats and design it for myself
- Calling my to-do list 'exciting projects' instead
- Being feminine in everything I do
- Sipping hot tea and perusing my style files for a break
- Dressing 'Paris sexy' – using that thought when I am choosing what to wear
- Cleansing my face with coconut oil and a hot flannel
- Having 'a week of no guilt' – I choose what I want to do
- Taking my time to do things
- Letting my life be easy
- Suspending thought and relaxing my body
- Letting go of the past

~~

My final example (next) is a little pep talk I wrote to myself:

~~

'I love being organized! It fulfils a great need in me – for order, peace and calm. I shall always make time to tidy up, put things away, tidy loose ends, keep tasks up-to-date, declutter, use things up, make space, organize my surroundings and generally have my home and life 'exactly' the way I want it to be. That is a promise to myself. xx'

~~

That little paragraph is only 63 words long but filled a whole notebook page. It took less than five minutes to write, I'd guess, and the payoff was immense. I know I would have felt so calm and content after writing that, and snuggled into bed to drift off to sleep. Re-reading it periodically reminds me what feels good, and to take the time to tidy my surroundings.

Whenever I let what is top-of-mind be the focus of my current happylist, the ideas flow beautifully. You know when it's easy to talk about your latest exciting project, goal or obsession? That's what your happylist notebook is for.

Benefits of happylists:

- You will start to feel happier and more content for no apparent reason.
- You will capture good ideas as they pop up, and not forget them.

- You will be reminded of all the goodness in your life.
- You will have the best book ever to read through if you're feeling a little flat.
- New ideas will be sparked from other ideas.
- You will start to feel a zingy, buzzy energy more often.

Your peaceful life tips:

- You don't need to go out and buy a notebook because I'm sure there is one you have been given, or bought in a sale, that you can go and use right now, and **start your own happylist**.

- Those **pretty little notebooks** that get tucked away unused because they are 'too good' to journal in **are absolutely perfect** for this task.

- I found one straight away and didn't have that frozen feeling about writing in a brand-new book, because I knew **this notebook would be filled with light and happiness**. A happylist notebook is not where you will be emptying out your head and working things out. It is a place where you will look forward to visiting and building up your own flavour of inspiration. I know you're going to love it!

Chapter 4.

The easy way to find out what you need to be happy

You may find that when you are doing something repetitive and methodical is when you do your best thinking. You might be out walking, hanging laundry on the clothesline, washing dishes or pulling weeds in the garden.

At these times things roll around in your head – issues you are pondering, or thinking how to sort something that is bothering you. It's a good thing to listen to your intuition but it can often seem difficult to get that flow going.

Umm, intuition, I'm waiting for you, are you even there?!

Something that has been immensely fun and helpful has been to ask my higher self questions. I say it out loud or in my mind, and ask her, 'Fiona, what shall we do about this?' I'd see what she thought of certain things and what suggestions she could offer. Amazingly, she has brought me great ideas which I might not have thought of 'myself'. The ideas just pop into my mind.

Along the same lines, another good way to access your intuition is to communicate with *your younger self*. I remember one time a few years back when I was feeling unsure of our future plans and even a little bit fearful. In my mind I hugged the five-year-old me and told her that it was going to be okay, and I would look after her no matter what. Incredibly, I felt comforted by this brief exchange.

Ever since then, I regularly check back in with this little girl to make sure she has everything she needs. I realize if you haven't heard of the concept before (or have, and decided that it's too woo-woo for you), you might skip past this chapter thinking it sounds ridiculous.

But I encourage you to try it at least once or twice, and hopefully you'll have excellent results like I did, because it's really nice to connect with those other versions of yourself. It feels comforting.

Ask her what she needs to be happy

One of my most fruitful conversations I had like this was to ask myself as a young girl what she needed to be happy.

Doing this a fun way to feel peaceful, grounded and content, and, it costs you nothing. Well, I guess that depends on what your little girl wants! But my little girl, little Fiona, had some soothing words for me when I asked her what she needed to be happy.

She told me she needs:

- Comfort and coziness.
- Routines and boundaries.
- Her books and pretty things, like her dolls.
- Yummy little dinners that also make her feel good.
- To play and run around.
- To go to the park and the beach.
- Creative time with her pencil and her book.

She told me she makes her own fun because she has such a vivid inner world of prettiness and imagination. She told me she loves being self-contained and in her own space. But she also needs me to make boundaries and routines for her when she's at home when no-one else is, because otherwise she would, as a young girl might, just wander around from room to room and probably get a bit bored.

When I help her though, when I make boundaries for her and put little routines into place, it makes her feel so happy, and it makes her feel safe. And she lets me know that she needs to feel safe because she has been scared, for no logical reason, but maybe it's the lack of boundaries and lack of security and lack of routine that has made her feel unsafe in the past.

She just needs me to take her in hand and guide her. Guide her to her ultimate happiness, guide her to find out what she loves doing the most. I hear that little girl, because deep inside I'm still the same person; that's my soul.

A message for you

My little girl wants to say something to you too. She wants to share her happiness, her creativity, and her self-sufficiency with you. She wants to show you, 'Look how much fun it can be when you create your own inner world to inspire you'. She wants to show you her world, and share it with you, because she knows you are lovely.

When I asked my little girl what it takes to make her happy, I didn't expect all that. And it wasn't me 'thinking', I just captured it.

It's the same with you. Can you imagine what *your* little girl might be waiting to talk to you about? Your younger self is *you*, and she wants you to notice her. Ask her what she wants to share. And if you can't hear what she has to say just yet, let her know that she is loved, safe, and will always be looked after by you. Maybe at that time, it's the most important and wonderful thing she can hear.

Your peaceful life tips:

- If this sounds like a fun exercise to you, ask your younger self what she needs to feel **happy, safe, and relaxed** – or use whatever words sound good to you.

- You can even **look at a picture of you when you were younger** if this helps, but for me, I could picture her straight away; she was definitely under ten, maybe under five, with bright white hair in a sticking-out bob.

- Include her in your life, and **have fun with her**!

Part 2:

Harmonious at Home

Chapter 5.

Creating peace and beauty in the home

Jane Austen said, 'There's nothing like staying at home for real comfort' and it's true. Home is the place where you can create a sanctuary, and surround yourself with your favourite colours, scents, sounds, and corners of beauty.

Yes, home is 'our happy place' for many of us. Even going away on vacation, I am almost more excited about coming home afterwards. I love going away but I love returning home more!

And I had the same conversation with a friend on the weekend. She and her husband were staying with us, and the night before they left I asked if she was excited about getting home. She said she definitely was, even though she'd had a lovely weekend away.

There is just something about feeling snug in your own space, and it doesn't matter how grand that space is. I was just as happy keeping our tiny first home spick and span as I am now. An enjoyable feeling comes from a clean and tidy space, along with personalized décor touches to delight your spirit.

Your own inspiring vision

In Marie Kondo's book 'The Life-Changing Magic of Tidying' there is a passage that I love for its soothing, inspirational quality. Marie wrote:

"One client in her twenties defined her dream as 'a more feminine lifestyle'. 'What do you mean by a "feminine lifestyle"?' I asked. She thought for a long moment before finally responding.
'Well, when I come home from work, the floor would be clear of clutter ... and my room as tidy as a hotel suite with nothing obstructing the line of sight. I'd have a pink bedspread and a white antique-style lamp. Before going to bed, I would have a bath, burn aromatic oils and listen to classical piano or violin while doing yoga and drinking herbal tea. I would fall asleep with a feeling of unhurried spaciousness.'
Her description was as vivid as if she actually lived that way. By the way, the client I described above does indeed enjoy post-bath aromatherapy, classical music and yoga. Freed from the depths of

disorder, she emerged to find the feminine lifestyle to which she aspired."

This quote sparked something inside me, and it was fun to ponder what kind of vision I had for our home. It would:

Be peaceful and calm
Have a sense of unhurried spaciousness
Be conducive to creativity (writing, sewing,
*   fashion designing)*
Be feminine and serene
Have free space everywhere you look, and
*   everything is put away*
Be as elegant as my favourite Langham Hotel

And in my ideal life, what kinds of things would I want to do at home I wondered?

Swim and sunbathe
Read books
Write books
Write my own inspiration
Sew/design clothes
Eat healthily
Have relaxing time every evening
Connect with friends and readers
Be inspired
Enjoy the outdoors and our garden
Feel proud of our surroundings
Enjoy our spacious and clutter-free home

It's an uplifting exercise to ask what your ideal vision for your home life is, and to ponder what you would most wish to do at home. Please note that we don't even have a swimming pool, and I don't go out in the sun much, but that just popped into my mind. So perhaps I might make more time for going for a swim at the beach or local pool in the summer, just as an example.

Each of us really can create more peace and beauty in our home, just by being intentional about how we want our home to look (and feel) like, and also listing out those things we picture ourselves doing in our ideal dream life. Why not live at least some of that dream life right now?

The benefits of being intentional with your living space and desired lifestyle is that you will bring about a sense of peacefulness and relaxation, and have a sense of fulfilment with your creativity. It will feel feminine and soothing, and life will have more ease. You will enjoy your home more, and likely feel less overwhelmed by your belongings and the stuck feeling of dusty corners etc, because you have an inspiring plan which is surprisingly easy to execute.

Add creativity into your day

Creativity makes the soul happy, no matter what form is most inviting to you, and brings both peace and beauty into the home. Do more of your best-loved hobby or artistic pursuit whether it's baking, quilting or writing poetry.

Aside from all the usual things that fill my day, I always make space for half an hour to read with a cup of coffee, and write as well. I have my style files to hand, and notebooks filled with ideas, goals and dreams.

You might say you have no time for all this flossy stuff, but I promise you can find some. Think about everything you do in a day, and see if there is a corner, a private space in your schedule, that you can book in with yourself for a time of contemplation towards your life of peace and beauty. Even fifteen minutes each day would be a start.

For me, I know it's social media I could replace. I hop onto Twitter to see what is happening in the world of politics and world news, and it sucks me right in! Before I know it almost an hour has passed, and I have nothing to show for it except perhaps frustration and disgust (and that's on a good day!)

Replacing something like that with my dreamy notebooks and style files is a worthwhile swap, and you might find the same.

It's so easy to just go with the flow and do things because they are there. But the real secret to creating a home and lifestyle that lifts you up and fits you 'just so', is to choose for yourself how you want to live and how you wish to spend your time.

It feels luxurious, wanton and frivolous to make time for your desires each day, but it's anything but. You will enhance your serenity, femininity, and inner soft happiness by doing this. And you are worth that. (Plus, your whole household will benefit, not just you, which is an excellent side effect don't you think?)

Go on, breathe out, be 'selfish' and think about creating more peace and beauty to surround yourself with. Do it now.

Your peaceful life tips:

- Consider the **ideal vision you have for your home life** and what kinds of things you imagine yourself doing in that vision.

- Work out cost-effective and time-friendly ways in which you can bring **elements of your vision** to life right now.

- Note down all forms of creativity you have ever engaged in, right back to when you were a child. Choose one or two to reignite and **start to be creative again**, even in a small way. Or, find something new that has always piqued your interest and do something with that.

- Show thoughts of selfishness the door and know that just because you are **taking care of your soul** doesn't mean you are neglecting anyone else – you are doing just the opposite.

Chapter 6.

Cozy domesticity

I used to follow a lovely blog called 'The Quiet Home' which isn't there anymore, but I remember it being the most relaxing place to visit. The UK-based writer talked about her simple home life: daily routines, the soft whoosh-whoosh of the washing machine going, and how much she enjoyed tending her home.

There is something so calming about changing your mindset when doing domestic duties. When you don't resist your chores or try to rush, but simply enjoy the routines and rhythms of everything that has to be done, time passes companionably.

It's almost meditative in a way (as I mentioned at the beginning of Chapter 4 – 'The easy way to find out what you need to be happy'), which is a good thing if you are someone who never seems to want to meditate. Perhaps you'd far rather handwash a pile of dishes or fold washing than count your breaths.

And they have the same outcome, because you do feel peaceful and grounded when you take your time to do things around the house, and do them to the best of your ability, in a relaxed manner.

I feel grateful and thankful for many things in my life, including that I enjoy my home so much. I have always loved tidying and prettifying where I live, whether it is my own home like now; a rented home; or even when I lived with my sister and two other girls before I met my husband, and the only space which was absolutely mine was my bedroom. I still remember what a haven it was back then.

I could be social and have fun with my housemates, and have my private time too. I kept my room clean and tidy, with a comfortable bed and all my books and perfumes on the shelves. It was decorated in a simple and soothing way, with my favourite colours around me. It was an inspiring refuge at a difficult time after my divorce.

It was here that I dreamed of the next phase of my life and wrote out my wish list of how I wanted to live, and who with. Nowadays I have more than I could ever have imagined, and I know there is still goodness to come.

That's the thing about life, it keeps on becoming more fabulous – but only if you expect it to. Louise Hay said that each decade of her life got better and better, and it did. When I read this, I decided on the spot that I was claiming it for myself as well. May I suggest you do too? It's the only way to live!

Enjoying simple routines

Today I am at home doing laundry, and going out later to pick up some groceries. We're in the middle of a spring downpour, complete with dark clouds and thunder. It was sunny this morning, so I got to take two happy dogs for a walk, and now I am cozy at home enjoying the feeling of getting tidied up – not for anything special, just daily organization.

I don't always find it easy getting started, but the feeling during and after straightening up the house, putting things away etc brings so much pleasure. It's such a nice feeling to be warm and snug inside while it's stormy outside and brings another level of satisfaction to homemaking.

No matter the humbleness of where I have lived, I have always been aware of the inner contentment that can be gained from putting a room to rights. I find it incredible that you can make a space look one-hundred-percent better without spending a cent.

If you also feel good in a tidy home, perhaps these thoughts are enough to change your mindset around housework and straightening up so that you actually look forward to doing it. (I know for me it almost seems like a minor miracle!)

Why not enjoy any given day of cozy domesticity and be grateful for it?

Tiny doses of happiness

Many years ago I read a magazine article which has stuck with me. The author, delving into how to be happy, said that it comes in small doses. When she was young, she thought she would be happy when she was a grown-up and that happiness would coat her life 'like a blanket of snow, covering everything in sight with a dazzling, seamless beauty'.

Now she is an adult, she knows this isn't the truth, and that happiness is more likely to be found *in the little things*. Things such as:

- Changing from high heels to slippers when she arrives home.
- Eating a piece of chocolate.
- Watching a funny television show.
- Reading a short story.
- Hugging.
- Wiping the crumbs from the kitchen counter.

I agree with all of these, and it's so true, they do make you feel happier. I was inspired to make my own list too. At any time, these things are guaranteed to lift my mood.

- Clearing the dining table of 'stuff'. Putting it all back where it belongs.
- Ditto the living room. Straightening it up.
- Enjoying a hydrating glass of water.

- Re-watching a favourite television program or movie.
- Reading or re-reading a fun and enjoyable chick lit book.
- Going for a walk.
- Enjoying the house after I have vacuumed and dusted.
- Hanging laundry on the line and then bringing it in to fold after a sunny day.
- Using up the last of something – body lotion then recycling the bottle, or vegetables in the fridge for a slow-cooker meal or soup.
- Putting a casserole in the Le Creuset and then enjoying the aroma as it cooks.
- Decluttering and organizing a drawer or cupboard.
- Washing the dishes by hand.
- Finishing off one job before starting another, rather than multi-tasking.
- Changing the bathroom hand towel frequently so it is always clean and dry.

Many of these things are *tiny* (clean hand towels?) that you think they couldn't possibly make much difference, but they do. And it will be different for each of us what those little 'happy touches' are.

With the world being such a place of turmoil, both man-made and with natural disasters, it is sometimes easy to feel scared or fearful for the future. It's very important to keep our home as our sanctuary of peace and order – our welcoming oasis to come back to.

And by giving out an energy of positivity and calm, we not only keep ourselves healthy and happy, but it affects others around us in a good way too.

We do what we can for those close to us who are in need of help, or by donating to charities, but it's not going to do anyone any good if we neglect ourselves. By taking small bites of happiness where we can, we will more enjoy this precious, short life we have been gifted.

Your peaceful life tips:

- When you have household tasks to do, **perform them with a bright spirit**. Do them with love for you and your family, and your pets too. When I have to empty the dishwasher (which I plan to do as soon as I finish this chapter), I will change my mindset to one of appreciation for my family of two people and four pets. And the fact that I have a dishwasher as well!

- And my second tip is that I try to **do things as quickly and efficiently as possible**. Yes, I do things in an unhurried manner, but I also remind myself not to dawdle or multi-task. It feels far better to finish one job and then go on to the next, and have one task completed entirely.

- Think about all the little things you can do around the home which will **increase your contentment factor**. When you look, you will find many.

Chapter 7.

Your bedroom is your sanctuary

Our bedroom is probably the room in the house that is most important to our wellbeing. We spend so much time in there! Between sleeping, loving, getting ready for bed, waking up in the morning, bathing, and dressing for the day, it's a place that has a big effect on us.

Our bedroom is the last thing we see at night and the first thing we see in the morning. This is why it is so important to have a cleanly furnished, restful haven which will support our serenity. We want our bedroom to enhance our daily life, not add to the stress.

The fascinating thing too, is that we often put our bedroom last in the priority queue behind other more public areas of our home, simply because fewer people will ever see our bedroom.

You don't need a complete makeover if your budget is tight or want to start beautifying your bedroom straight away. There are tons of things you can do for free to make your bedroom a restful haven and a place to truly enjoy going to bed each night.

How to give your bedroom a makeover with no money

There is an English television show that I used to watch called 'Perfect Housewife'. It was a decluttering/makeover show but no money was spent to get the results; the contestants had to do everything themselves.

With each episode I used to marvel at the huge difference decluttering and cleaning made to a room. This program was excellent housework motivation because it really inspired me to get going!

Borrowing from 'Perfect Housewife', you can do wonders to increase your bedroom's peaceful energy by doing the same. Firstly, by **removing everything from your bedroom** that is not related to sleep, love or relaxation.

So... the treadmill? No. The clothing drying rack by the window? No. I even consider a television a no-no in the bedroom, but I can imagine I am in the minority here. I just think they are the biggest passion killers! Of course, if you already have one in your bedroom, it might be hard to give it up, so keep it if you love it.

If you have a bed on legs, with space underneath rather than a base, is there anything under there? Feng shui says not to have anything stored under your bed, so ideally it would be a clear space. But I understand storage is often at a premium, so if you do have anything under your bed, make sure it is appropriate, tidy and dust-free.

And if you never pull those things out, do you even need them? Why not see if you can store them elsewhere, or declutter them all together.

And, **clean off your bedside tables**. I used to pile everything up beside my bed so it was easy to grab. A teetering stack of books, body butter, hand cream, lip balm and at least one drink (water, tea...); you could barely see the top of the cabinet!

I had an awakening when I heard Colin Cowie on the Oprah show and he said he put everything from the top of his bedside table into the top drawer. Items are still to hand, but you don't have to look at them. I did this straight away and it worked so well. I had to clean that drawer out of junk first, but it was a small drawer so didn't take long.

I then enjoyed setting it up with dividers and all the little things I wanted to keep in there. My lotions, of course, plus my pretty bookmark collection, pens and little notebooks. On the top I kept one book (the book I was currently reading) along with my water bottle, plus the lamp.

It was such a calming tableau to greet me at night, and still is.

While you are doing all of this, **give your bedroom an extra-good clean**. Pull the bed out and vacuum behind it. Wipe the skirting boards with a damp cloth. Vacuum your mattress next time you change the sheets. Clean your light fittings and lamps. Using a sticky roller on the fabric shade shows you how much dust has accumulated.

Having a simply furnished bedroom that is lovely and clean will feel so different to before. It will also be easier to keep tidy. The more you have in a room, the more there is to clean and keep nice, so make it easy on yourself and give yourself the gifts of spaciousness and ease.

Make your bed with care each day

This one little thing will *transform* how you see your bedroom. Before I started taking care with how I made our bed, it was such a begrudging use of my time. After all, we'd only just get back in at night and mess it up, wouldn't we?

It was rare that I wouldn't make the bed at all, but I remember there were days when I pulled the top cover up and piled the pillows and cushions back on, glad that this dreaded chore was behind me.

These days, I still don't look forward to making my bed, but I just get in there and do it. And it only takes five minutes, even when I take my time. As with many things, getting started is the hardest part.

But when I do the little extras, such as smooth out the fitted sheet and make sure all the corners are snugly tucked down, pull up the top sheet and duvet, blanket, fold the top sheet back over everything, then put our pillows up plus the European pillows and two decorative cushions, the effect on the room is huge.

Our bedroom looks luxurious, lodge-like, and serene. It really is the single most important thing you can do to improve the look – and feel – of your bedroom on a daily basis. And it's wonderful climbing into bed at night, letting yourself sink into the smooth bottom sheet. It's a very comforting feeling to have your bed support you.

When I did regular yoga classes many years ago, we would do the rest pose at the end, lying on our back on the floor. I remember the teacher always saying, 'Let the floor support you', which I thought was lovely. It really did feel different to just lying on the floor. So, when you are resting, let your bed support you.

When you take the time to make your bed with care, there is the aesthetic aspect – your room looks great every time you happen to be in there, but there is also the self-care aspect. You are taken care of at night. You feel pampered. Even when it was you who made the bed.

Your bedroom is the one place you can truly feel private. Make it your peaceful retreat from the world and see how it relaxes you every night, and refreshes you every morning.

Your peaceful life tips:

- If there is a lot to sort in your bedroom before it becomes your peaceful sanctuary, **start with something small**. Clear off your bedside tables and see how nice it looks, or remove one item that shouldn't be in the room. Look at that lovely empty space now that the washing basket has been emptied and put back in the laundry room!

- **Ask yourself inspiring questions**, such as:

  How can I make our bedroom a beautiful, luxurious retreat?
  How can I make the most of our bedroom?
  How can I make our bedroom a restful haven?

  Take note of the little answers that pop into your mind. Even just reading these questions relaxes me; it's fabulous how the mind works!

Chapter 8.

Creating a spa atmosphere at home

One of my favourite ways to feel relaxed and cosseted is to recreate the peaceful feeling of a beauty spa at home.

If you've ever been lucky enough to visit a spa, think about the peaceful ambiance created specially to relax you. It doesn't matter if it is a spa at a five-star hotel or a small local beauty therapist, it all comes down to the details.

When I visit such a place, I feel a sense of serenity as soon as I step in the door. Peace and order soothe my mind and I can feel my shoulders relax.

Soft music is playing, the space is free of clutter, and displays are minimal and feminine. Lighting is dimmed; perhaps there is a lamp or even fairy lights glowing instead of an overhead ceiling light. Décor colours are harmonious and often light in tone. There is an essential oil diffuser bubbling away, dispensing lavender and orange to create a pleasing fragrance. You absorb a sense of stillness simply by being there.

Luxury and relaxation at home

Conjuring up this dreamy spa atmosphere can inspire you to apply some of those same principles to your own home so you can infuse your everyday with a refreshing calm. You will be inspired to:

- Tidy things away to their rightful place.

- Declutter items that were there just because they've always been there (and you weren't particularly fussed on them anyway).

- Organize items on display to make them look more attractive. Perhaps grouping regularly used items onto a small tray in the bathroom.

- Think, speak and move in a soft and measured way. Be intentional. Pad around the home in soft socks, or with house shoes on.

- Dress simply and elegantly, with your hair pulled back into a ponytail or chignon if you want to feel extra neat and productive.

- Take the time to apply a face mask or moisturize your feet. You could apply a mud mask a few times each month, and massage your feet nightly with a creamy body lotion. It feels so luxurious and soothing yet costs very little. Wear hotel slippers or bed socks while it absorbs.

- Be organized with your time and not rush from task to task. Do one thing then continue onto the next. Remind yourself to move in an unhurried manner. There is no hurry. You are calm. You have the time.

- Add more table lamps to your décor; there is no rule that says you can only have one per room!

- Have dimmers put on your living room and bedroom light switches.

- Have a playlist of relaxing music (you can look up my 'Dior relaxing music' playlist on Spotify, where I recreated a CD I was given while working at Christian Dior – it was played when beauty consultants gave their clients a special Dior facial treatment).

- Have pretty touches such as flowers or even a sculptural branch in a bud vase.

- Open the bedroom windows when you make your bed in the morning. And after tidying everything away finish off your housekeeping duties with a fragrant spritz of something light and floral.

- Scent the air in other rooms of the house with an essential oil diffuser, scented candle, or wax melt depending on your mood. Open your windows often. The combination of fresh air with a fragrant aroma is blissful. Some are sensitive to fragrance and prefer none; just go with what makes you feel best.

'The Gurus' Guide to Serenity' by Laurel and Sharon House has some great tips on being spa-like at home. I borrowed it from the public library a long time ago and remembered how lovely it was, so ordered it second-hand online. Happily, it was just as good as I remembered. Even flicking through a few pages relaxes me. Your library might still have a copy to browse to see if you feel the same.

Tidy and neat

You may also find that being inspired by the orderly and calming inspiration of a spa establishment helps you to find the motivation to deal with cluttery messes and restore a peaceful vista to your surroundings.

Our eyes subconsciously pick up on everything around us, so if we have bits and pieces lying around, our serenity is threatened. I often think to myself that the energy drained by noticing something unfinished is more than if I had expended the energy to deal with it in the first place. This thought encourages me to do something straight away if it's a small task. The payoff is so satisfying.

Feng Shui is useful in creating a spa-like atmosphere at home too. There is something about the precise placement of furniture making a room feel calm, and being free of clutter that links both. It is being purposeful with your energy, your movement, and your thoughts.

I'm no Feng Shui expert, but the basic principles can definitely calm the mind and will lend a relaxing spa feeling to your home:

- Clean and tidy your space – declutter items you no longer care for.

- Try not to have too much packed into one room.

- Arrange furniture so that the flow of a space is pleasing – you want it to be easy to move around the room.

- As much as possible, have a bedroom furnished with only those things which promote relaxation, (as detailed in Chapter 7 – 'Your bedroom is your sanctuary').

- Clear any clutter from doorways, especially if something inhibits you from opening or shutting a door completely.

- Fix anything that is broken, shabby or squeaky. If it is not fixable, consider throwing it away or recycling it.

- Keep your front entranceway welcoming, by dusting cobwebs, sweeping it regularly, and with plants kept watered and healthy-looking.

- Use your front door as the main entrance, not a back or side door.

- Get rid of things that are stained and cannot be cleaned.

- Keep the toilet seat down. I started doing this almost twenty years ago because we had a cat who would drink from the toilet bowl. Now I prefer it because it's nicer to see, plus it has become a habit.

- Have your bed located in a place where it feels 'safe' compared to the position of the door. You want to be able to see your door from bed, not have it be behind or to the side of you, for example. It just feels better.

- And clean your windows inside and out! You will be able to 'see' better in life.

I don't do the whole Feng Shui thing fully, but I can certainly feel when a space feels welcoming, peaceful and serene, so there must be something to it. All of the guidelines above will help your home feel better, and it will be easier to live in.

Feeling relaxed and at peace does wonders for your health, both mental and physical. If recreating the feeling of a resort spa in your private surroundings helps with that, why not try it out?

Your peaceful life tips:

- **Does the thought of a spa inspire you to tidy and simplify?** Or perhaps take the time to give yourself a mud mask and pampering foot massage? What is something you could do right now?

- **Investigate the simplest of Feng Shui cures**. Use my tips above, or there are plenty of 'easy Feng Shui' or 'best Feng Shui tips' online if you use these search phrases. Often they are simple little tweaks which make a big difference to the feel of a room. If nothing else, they will make it a little bit more fun to tidy up.

Part 3:

Your Feminine Soul

Chapter 9.

Infuse your life with rose-tinted beauty

Back in 2010 when I started my blog 'How to be Chic', I wanted it to be an elegant, feminine place to write, that I looked forward to visiting. To give a soft, dreamy glow, I chose the pink background colour which I still love today. It's a pink that isn't too babyish, but a blush pink with a touch of sophistication.

Then, when my husband and I started having 'staycations' at the Langham Hotel once or twice a year when we still lived in Auckland, I saw that their trademark pink touches were almost the same shade. They often paired their pink with gold, which is particularly elegant – and French – in my mind, as I have seen photos of beauty boutiques and perfumiers decorated in a pink/gold combination.

Apparently, the Ritz Hotel in Paris painted the walls in their rooms a subtle peach-pink because it throws a flattering light onto the skin. I don't know if they still do this, but I've always remembered the detail because it sounds so luxurious, yet simple. Sheets in a delicate blush pink would be delightful too, and excellent Feng Shui for love and romance in the bedroom.

All these divine pink touches I have noticed over time have led me to intentionally cultivate more pink in my life because it has such an uplifting and beautifying effect on my spirit. Even if you are a self-proclaimed 'not a pink person', surely the sight of a bouquet of pink roses can't fail to have an instinctive effect on your happiness?

I'd like to share with you some petite ways to enjoy a feminine touch of pink (without demasculinising your home so much that your husband feels like he is living in Barbara Cartland's boudoir).

You could have:

- Pale pink bar soap in the shower (this feels very 'old Hollywood').

- Soft bath towels and face flannels – our current towels are shades of charcoal and dark taupe, and I have a mad desire to buy a pair of bright fuchsia pink towels which I think would look so fun in our simple white bathroom.

- A luxurious bathrobe in a feminine shade – satin is nice for summer, and fluffy fleece robes are delicious to snuggle into after bathing in the winter.

- Pretty and feminine journals to write in.

- Divinely soft pink scuff slippers – I buy a new pair every winter, and they are so comforting to wear around the house. Alternatively, fluffy mohair socks to keep your feet warm in the winter.

- New pyjamas or a nightdress in a becoming shade of pink – when I needed to replace a few nightwear items I specifically chose the most feminine choices, either in plain colours or with abstract floral prints. My nightwear collection looks so pretty all together, and it's a pleasure to change into my pyjamas at night.

- Lingerie in pale or blush pink – I made this change for my light-coloured clothing instead of the beige or nude I usually chose.

- Pens - I have slim metal pens picked up at the Langham Hotel; they are pink with a gold print on. And if I have to buy a pen, I'll choose the prettiest looking one available.

- Pastel-coloured writing paper and stationery – you can find paper, little note cards, and general greeting cards to keep on hand.

- Padded satin coat hangers in soft, feminine colours or prints.

- A rose or other flower in a bud vase – I love bud vases because you can pick a few flowers from your garden and the look is totally lush. You don't need to know how to arrange flowers either!

- A floral cup and saucer or ultra-feminine mug to drink your tea from.

I bought a pair of beautiful floral English Kew Garden cups from a thrift store for $2 each – they looked to be brand new. A whizz through the dishwasher and they were 'new to us'. I thought it would be just me using them because they are festooned with pretty flowers in feminine shades, but my husband Paul often chooses them when making us a cup of tea.

Men appreciate feminine touches too, more than you would think – Paul often says how he loves the small details I bring to our home, such as lighting candles every night etc.

Even music can have a colour – when I play spa music softly in my bedroom at night, it has an iridescent, almost shimmering quality while I am washing my face and having quiet time before bed.

Imagine how nice feminine loungewear would be in soft shades of rose too – the kind of clothes you change into for the evening – they aren't quite public clothes, but not pyjamas either. Currently my loungewear is black, grey marle, and black-and-white stripes. When I replace items as needed, I will do so in softer, prettier colours.

There is a feminine shade for all of us

If pink doesn't have pleasing connotations for you, why not consider seashell, blush, rose, peony, fuchsia, cerise, lavender, lilac, petal, mauve or any other nuance that you could intentionally add more of into your life as your feminine touchstone.

Choose a soft colour that makes your heart happy and, when you need something, why not choose a pretty, feminine colour?

It doesn't even need to be in the pink/purple range. Another colour that is delightfully feminine is pale sea glass blue/green; this would be a beautiful shade to use as your feminine accent colour. The light-coloured packaging of Estée Lauder products is this exact shade. I even saved a small sample box flattened out as inspiration.

Take a look at brands you are drawn to and see what their colours are. Borrow them if they make you feel happy. Companies spend a lot of money with colour specialists coming up with their brand's look and feel, and a big part of that is colour.

I read that Estée Lauder herself originally chose the soft blue/green shade for her jars paired with gold lids, because she thought the combination would blend well with most bathroom decors.

The more you surround yourself with feminine touches, the softer and more relaxed you will feel on a daily basis. We take beauty in through our eyes and other senses, so why not intentionally cultivate feminine surroundings for a serene life?

Your peaceful life tips:

- How do you feel about pink? Or perhaps you might have a different **feminine accent colour that you love**? Look for ways you can introduce more of it into your life.

- Don't try to eradicate all traces of femininity from your home in case you think your husband (and any other males you happen to live with) will feel uncomfortable. As mentioned about my husband, I have noticed **men appreciate a lady's touch in the home**. It sounds old-fashioned to even say 'a lady's touch', but men can't help being drawn to beauty, just as we are. They just never think to do those things. But trust me, they will notice and like them.

Chapter 10.
Boudoir time

One of the nicest ways to feel feminine and relaxed is to indulge in 'boudoir time' on a regular basis.

I heard the term from author Anne Barone originally. In her *Chic & Slim* book series, Anne mentions that chic French women take regular 'boudoir time'. This means they withdraw to their 'boudoir' to take stock, recharge, and spend quiet time alone.

This is such an important thing for our wellbeing, and something that many of us forget about. I know I can forget too when life gets busy, and that's exactly when it will do me the most good!

The good news is that you can do it at home, in private. You can start tonight. It doesn't need to take long, and once a week will do wonders for your sense of inner peacefulness.

How I do my boudoir time

I usually have boudoir time in the evening, by retiring to our bedroom earlier than normal. All going well this is between 8pm and 9pm, if we have had our dinner early enough and are cleaned up. I leave my husband happily watching his television program in the living room.

It helps to start with a tidy bedroom, so if there are a few things lying around I will put them away. Our bed is already neatly made, with pillows and cushions arranged in a pleasing way. All laundry is in the hamper, and clothes are hung up and put away. I turn the bedside lamps on so there is a soft glow rather than the overhead light and start a relaxing music playlist.

Part of my boudoir time is taking my time removing makeup, washing my face, and perhaps applying a clay mask. Firstly, I take my eye makeup off with micellar water and a cotton pad. I then massage in facial cleansing oil, taking my time to mimic the kinds of massage movements that I remember from having facials. I don't have any set ways, just what is gentle and feels good.

Once my makeup is emulsified with the oil, I'll run a basin of fairly warm water (as hot as I can put my hands into) and wet a face flannel, wringing it out until it's almost dry. Cleansing the oil off with a hot flannel is blissful! I swish the flannel around in the hot water, wring it out, and repeat rinsing my face twice more.

After this I will either use my Clarisonic facial brush or an exfoliating cream, and follow up with a mask. At the moment I love to apply a clay mask on my t-zone, with coconut oil on my cheeks as a moisturizing mask.

Once the mask is on, I spread myself out on our bed with my journals, a book, or a soothing magazine such as *Victoria*. Alternatively, I may choose one of my style files to browse through – I keep printed-out blog inspiration or torn-out magazine articles in clear display-pocket folders. I spend this time reading, dreaming, and soaking in the feeling of tranquility.

It doesn't particularly matter which material I browse, it's just whatever I am in the mood for at the time. The most important thing is that I select something which promotes a sense of quietude.

I also have a glass of water or herbal tea on the bedside table and sip this while I read.

After about 15-20 minutes I wash my mask off and then change the water in the basin to give a final rinse with clean water and enjoy putting on my serum, night cream and eye cream. I apply a creamy body lotion to my neck, decolletage, arms, shoulders, wrists and hands, and feet. I also apply lavender essential oil balm to my wrists.

I pack up all my journals, books and magazines and put them away, then settle into bed with my current book.

Can you feel how relaxing boudoir time could be, even just from reading about it? Imagine how good you will feel from actually doing it. There are so many benefits to boudoir time!

- It is far more conducive to sleeping well than watching television or being on the computer.
- It is a very relaxing prelude to drifting off to sleep.
- You won't be tempted to stay up late for no reason if you have boudoir time to look forward to.
- Your eyes won't get scratchy from being on the computer close to bedtime.
- You will feel like you are living your idealistic dream life when you do this at least once or twice a week.
- You will feel like a lady of leisure.

- It feels meditative which is good if you don't do any other form of meditation.
- You can actually *feel* your muscles relax when you turn on the gentle spa music.
- If you journal during this time you will be amazed at the great insights and ideas you come up with.
- There is no cost – it is completely free to do.
- It slows down time, punctuates your week and stops one day sliding into the next.
- You will sleep very well after this calming wind-down to bedtime.
- It will feel like you take your self-care seriously when you make time to do this.
- It is a very enjoyable hour or so.
- It will feel feminine and 'French' to pamper yourself in this way.

Choose one night this week to indulge in some boudoir time and feel how enjoyable it is and how well you sleep. You will be a convert too!

Your peaceful life tips:

- In the evening is my favourite time, but **yours might be on a Sunday morning**, before breakfast, or any time that suits you and your schedule.

- Your boudoir time might look different to mine too. I don't particularly enjoy baths, but **a nightly bath** might be part of your relaxing time.

- Consider **your boudoir time as a sacred ritual** and *revel* in it. Soak it in. Remember how much you enjoy it and give gratitude for this time.

- If you have found any new ideas in this chapter, add one or two into your relaxing time and **see how they fit**. You might do them once and never again, or they may become a new favourite part of your regime.

Chapter 11.

The restorative powers of femininity

Within each of us there is a blend of the masculine and feminine. The masculine side of us is the 'doing' part, and the feminine side is the 'being'.

The feminine is our natural state as females, however we also need to access our masculine for that 'get things done' power. Otherwise we might sit around being floaty and drifty, just 'being'. Relaxing is definitely a good thing, just not all the time. A balance of both is the goal.

Some of us – I know I definitely do – spend more time in our masculine than is good for us. We are all go, go, go and wonder why we can sometimes feel so tired and out of sorts. We have been spending so much time in our masculine and give very little attention to our feminine during these periods.

There was one particular episode I recall vividly which occurred after the release of one of my books. I'd been so focused on everything I needed to do to get that book out that once it was all over, I crashed. I felt like I could sleep for a week; I wasn't motivated to do *anything,* and I was completely burnt out.

I had spent a prolonged amount of time in my masculine, and my feminine was rebelling!

After the book was released my body felt free to relax and so she did - bigtime. It's a little bit like that phenomena where people catch a cold as soon as they go on vacation. Their body knows it's safe to relax now, and an illness manifests to enforce that rest.

It wasn't that I was particularly stressed before the book was released, nor burning the midnight oil or anything like that, but it must be a natural response to a time of intense concentration. I'm sure students feel the same after exams are over, or at work after someone has completed a big project.

In the past I might have eaten my favourite sugar/ chocolate/ ice-cream/ popcorn/ potato chip treats to feel more normal but realized this doesn't help anything. Those snacky treat foods tasted like exactly what I thought I needed at the time, but they were false friends because I felt wretched afterwards.

Can you relate to this whole scenario?

Nourish your femininity

It helps to recognize the strange feeling for what it is – that you have been ignoring your feminine side in preference to the driving masculine energy which has helped you get a lot done in a short period of time. Or even a long time – perhaps you habitually live in your masculine and ignore your feminine, considering that side of yourself as optional and frivolous. But at what cost?

If this sounds like you, it helps to **be gentle with yourself** and treat yourself almost like a convalescing patient – it feels good to do this. Going to bed earlier than usual is extremely helpful; at these times we are likely getting by on less sleep than we need.

You might still have important or urgent tasks to complete, so write them all down and tick them off one by one over the following days. As nice as it would be to just throw everything to the side, we still need to function in the world while we rebuild ourselves.

Moving forward, the key to your wellbeing is that you **focus on your femininity**.

For me, as I mentioned, I recognized that the flattened feeling I was experiencing was from being in my masculine for weeks on end as I concentrated on completing my book – all the editing and re-reading work. Before that I had a nice blend of feminine 'being' and masculine 'doing' as I wrote the book, but at some stage I put my foot on the accelerator to get it completed and ready for publishing.

Once the book was out though, and I started taking better care of myself, I welcomed the feminine back in, finding these tips particularly useful:

By learning from the past – there was no need to overwork myself (and my mind). There was just some voice inside that *thought* I had to and it was whipping me on. But I have plenty of evidence from releasing other books that exhaustion and burnout is not necessary, and I have remembered that.

By reading books on my Kindle – Since I write non-fiction, I love to read novels and novellas to relax. My husband Paul thinks it is so funny that I sit at my computer writing my books, then come out into the living room to relax with a drink in the late afternoon and... read a book on my Kindle – like a busman's holiday (if you haven't heard that saying, it refers to 'a holiday or form of recreation that involves doing the same thing that one does at work')!

By focusing on grooming – blow-drying my hair, using lots of lovely, scented moisturizer, putting on perfume, and painting my nails - feeling feminine and pretty.

By partaking in boudoir time – as detailed in Chapter 10 – 'Boudoir time'.

By spending more time with my husband – of course, writing my books is a good thing, but I can feel like a neglectful wife if I am glued to the computer in preference to being with him. We relax at home a lot, and do household projects, or if we go out it might be for lunch or coffee, or a movie at the theatre.

By enjoying my closet – playing around creating outfits, wearing my nicest clothes, and accessorizing more with necklaces, plus trying new makeup looks.

By tending to our home and enjoying homemaking – doing more than just the basics. It is relaxing to indulge in some rearranging, organizing, decluttering, changing the look of a room, that kind of thing.

By handcrafting – my favourites such as sewing and knitting. They always get put aside 'because I'm busy', but I so enjoy playing around creating something.

By prettying up my makeup area – cleaning all my makeup items, sharpening pencils and washing my makeup brushes. From working behind the scenes in the high-end cosmetic industry (I was in the Christian Dior head office here in New Zealand), I can tell you that the beauty counter staff spent a lot of time cleaning their displays to make them look enticing. It was drilled into them to clean and polish their counters, displays and products every day.

When you do the same, putting your makeup on the next day with your 'new' makeup and washed brushes will give you such a buzz, and it truly will make you feel like you have been shopping for new makeup. All your products will seem new and exciting!

(I use a bottle of perfume as the cleaning agent (one of my least favourites to wear but still pretty to sniff) and a clean knit rag (from worn-out tee-shirts). I clean the outside of each case and even open up and clean the mirror and all around the eyeshadows or blusher.)

By buying or picking flowers – I often forget about flowers in the home; I just never think to do them. But when I do find an inexpensive bunch or fill a bud vase with something from our garden, it makes the world of difference.

In the past I've walked past flower displays at the supermarket and deemed them extravagant, not really necessary and even wasteful. I decided to change my mind to view them as 'feminine and luxurious'. I have started to make them a regular thing, and could even look at it as an elegant swap: I spend a few dollars on flowers instead of 'treat' foods. There are no calories in flowers and they are far better for me than processed junk!

But mostly, I think I'll just remember to pick flowers from the garden. I don't have the biggest garden in the world and I'm not a natural born gardener, but there is always something to find.

After choosing from this lovely list of enticing offerings, you will find that it's not too long before you start feeling uplifted. You might also make the decision for the future not to upset your equilibrium so much when completing projects. It's a good goal to have: achieve what you want to achieve without knocking yourself out of kilter along the way. As I already mention, I certainly learned 'what not to do' after that book was finally published.

Listen for the signs

If you are busy, busy, busy, you might find yourself being drawn to femininity and anything feminine. It is a natural response if you have been action-oriented and not had as much of an opportunity to slow down.

You may find you have pushed aside the things you used to enjoy pottering around with (they will probably seem too 'slow' for you when you are charging ahead on your goals, schedule or to-do list).

When I come across a woman or a girl who is very feminine in herself, her energy calls to me and I want to create that for myself. From following the *Downton Abbey* series, I loved watching Cora, Lady Grantham. Her voice and mannerisms are soft and gentle and she is very forgiving, but she's not weak or pathetic. As much as I think her daughter Lady Mary is beautiful and elegant, I would prefer to have the softness of Cora.

You may find that you notice when a lady or a situation is very feminine, and it means you could be missing that in your life right now, so you are picking up on it. It's wonderful that not only is it a reminder to be more feminine, but that you can do so instantly. And you're not just doing it for others, you're doing it for yourself, first and foremost. But your loved ones gain the benefit as well. It's a lovely awareness.

Your peaceful life tips:

- It's not a bad thing to spend time in your masculine energy; as I mentioned, it helps get things sorted. But **to not spend any time in your feminine is when the going gets rough**. If you're anything like me you will start acting out in small and perhaps not-so-small ways: being grumpy with yourself and everyone else around you because you feel resentful, treating yourself in unhelpful ways with fattening foods and online shopping that you don't even really want.

- Take the tips from this chapter and **nurture your femininity**. Your feminine being will help you feel relaxed and happy, and still with the ability to function in the real world. Embrace the beautiful blend of feminine and masculine energies to **create your own incredible flavour of life**.

Chapter 12.

Simple ways to be more feminine in your everyday life

Introducing small pockets of femininity into your day helps everything run smoother. You will feel more ladylike and life is enjoyable – even when you are doing mundane tasks.

In this chapter I go through my favourite ways of using the five senses to cultivate femininity. Looking at all the senses diversifies our pleasures, otherwise we can easily go to our default sense (which is taste for many of us – chocolate or pie!)

By taste

Fresh fruit. Instead of a biscuit (cookie) or cake for afternoon tea, wash and slice an apple or other piece of fresh fruit and savour it piece by piece from a pretty plate. Water-rich food is so deliciously plumping (in a hydrating way) to the cells of your body, and you will feel refreshed and light afterwards. Add several raw almonds or a slice of cheese for a balanced snack.

Herbal tea. Find an herbal tea you like the look of and enjoy it daily. There are many different teas around – *so many*. If you are not a fan of traditional herbal teas such as peppermint or chamomile, try a fruit tea.

When I settle down for a morning of writing, I like to make myself an herbal tea and top it up with hot water when I get down to the half-way mark, many times over. 'One' cup lasts me hours! It's nice to sip on *plus* I get good hydration plus I don't snack when I am doing this. Win/win/win.

Petite sweet. Find a morsel that you can love in moderation, to enjoy something sweet to finish off a meal. I love bliss balls, and I find that one bliss ball with a small piece of dark chocolate goes well together. Similarly, a delicious pairing is a dried apricot with a piece of dark chocolate.

With my bliss balls I love that I have an alternative to dark chocolate for after meals and that it's quite a healthy alternative too. Yes, they are still high in fat and sugar but they are so rich you can happily eat just one in a sitting. Even though they're healthy, they're still a treat food. And that's the point of a petite sweet – something that is tiny and rich. You can find my recipe at the end of this chapter.

I always keep dark chocolate in the pantry, and if I have nothing else available, it's nice to let a piece melt on my tongue.

By sight

Appreciating art. I once read an interview with Terry Gunzberg, former YSL employee (she invented the iconic Touche Éclat radiant highlighter pen) and founder of bespoke makeup brand By Terry. In the interview I loved what she had to say about art. She has been collecting for years, a piece at a time, and she bought a small artwork with her first paycheck.

She said her mother took her to galleries when she was young, and that she gained an appreciation from that. I don't often go to galleries, but when I do, I enjoy viewing the paintings, particularly older ones. At high school I studied art history for a year and I can still remember details of the renaissance paintings we studied.

The study of art seems like such a feminine pursuit to me. There are many ways to be cultured and I choose art as one of mine. You may prefer something else such as live theatre or ballet.

Viewing beautiful images. I've mentioned *Victoria* magazine before, but leafing through a copy is like a feast for the eyes (I declutter most other magazines once I have read them, but not *Victoria*). My own personal and decor style is much simpler than the homes pictured, but I am always inspired to be more ladylike and refined afterwards.

Glossy picture books are the same - Vicki Archer's 'My French Life' and 'French Essence' transport me to Paris via stunning large-scale images, and her writing style allows me to dream. I love them both, but if I had to pick a favourite, I'd choose 'My French Life' by a pip.

And I adore both of Aerin Lauder's books – 'Beauty at Home', and 'Entertaining Beautifully'.

By scent

Wine tasting. Whenever my husband and I share a bottle of wine I love to smell the bouquet and pick out different notes. I actually think I have quite a good nose!

It's fascinating how many notes there are in wine, and a helpful thing to do is either read the description on the bottle to see if you can pick them out, or google that particular varietal to see what the common characteristics are. Doing this has helped me learn what to 'smell' for.

But just how is this feminine? When I sniff for wine notes, it feels a little bit artistic, a little bit slow-living. It's taking the time to notice the details, and that in itself feels feminine. Living life deliberately, moving graciously, taking your time, and not rushing.

Fragrance. Every day, no matter what I am doing, I wear perfume. Sometimes it is 'perfumey', sometimes it is a fresh and light 'skin scent'.

I also enjoy perfume oils, essential oil types and inexpensive fragrant oils such as from *The Body Shop*. I usually prefer a little more 'volume' than an oil can provide, however they are fantastic to wear at work or when you are getting into a car with someone and don't want to knock their socks off. I also wear them to bed, as I love to drift off to sleep with a light comforting fragrance on.

Another nice way to subtly fragrance yourself is with a perfumed body lotion. Some are so long-lasting that you don't need to add perfume.

Scented candles are quite commonplace these days, and beautiful of course, but for a change I like to burn incense too. There are pretty incenses you can get – I love rose, vanilla, 'fresh linen' and sandalwood. Lighting incense always gives me a relaxing yoga/spa retreat type feeling. My favourite brand for many years has been Satya, but I try other brands from time to time as well.

By sound

Classical music. The right kind of classical music instantly elevates the frequency of an environment. I used to think it was boring and old-fashioned when I was younger, and now, thankfully, I have grown into appreciating it. I love it when you walk into a hotel lobby and hear an elegant sounding violin concerto. One time a live harpist was playing in a hotel I was having afternoon tea at; it was so beautiful!

At home I have a playlist with lots of classical pieces which I have gradually curated to include only those that I love. If anything is too clangy, strident or cannony, I delete that track. As a result I now listen to a mix of soothing strings and calming adagios. I feel instantly more elegant and refined – and feminine – when I have music like this playing.

Having a lovely voice. In my book 'Thirty Chic Days', I mention that I strive to keep my voice pleasant. I have horrors of turning into a shrewish, screeching fishwife; so to avoid this I try to remember to walk into a room to talk to someone rather than yell for them, and endeavour to speak as much as necessary and not dominate the conversation. I don't always manage it, but at least I try, right?

And another thing: do you ever leave somewhere thinking, 'I couldn't stop talking; whatever must they think of me?' I do! Or rather, I did. I think (I hope) I am better at this now – a two-way conversation where you ask questions of others and actually listen to what they say. The 'two ears, one mouth' reminder is so on point, as always.

By touch

Choosing fabrics that feel nice against your skin. When a fabric is soft on your skin, it is easy to feel comforted. Some of it has to do with the quality and price of the fabric, but not always. I have inexpensive items that feel wonderful. It's not something you might see the link to straight away, but that you realize you don't particularly enjoy wearing a certain top, for example.

Having fabric touch your skin that is displeasing threatens your femininity because it makes you irritable. When I am like this, I tend to be more masculine by stomping, snapping, with harsh words etc, due to irritation.

Keeping your skin hydrated. I am a huge fan of moisturizing and do it now more than I ever have before. It's so important for both the health and appearance of your skin, and I think this is what sets us apart from men – having soft skin. It's a particularly feminine thing to do (you'd hardly ever see a man moisturizing his hands after washing them!) and I adore the ritual of my morning toilette where I moisturize my whole body after my shower.

Additional moisturizings throughout the day include:

Hand lotion or cream many times a day
Neck and décolletage before I go to bed
A thick cream on my feet each night

To supplement external moisturizing, keep your skin hydrated from the inside out by drinking plenty of water and eating water-rich foods (fresh fruit and non-starchy vegetables), and good fats such as raw nuts and avocados.

Whether it's internal or external, I don't believe you can hydrate your skin too much. You will never look back in life and think to yourself, 'I wish I hadn't drunk so much water over the years' or 'I wish I hadn't eaten so much fresh fruit in the past'!

I hope these 'feminine senses' tips have given you some new ideas to try, and I also hope that you enjoy my recipe below if you decide to make my bliss balls.

~~

Fiona's Bliss Ball recipe

1 cup dates
1/2 cup dried apricots
1 cup almond meal
2 tbsp coconut flakes (or desiccated coconut)
1 tbsp coconut oil
1-2 tbsp peanut butter

Whizz the dates and apricots in a food processor then add the other ingredients and whizz again. If you don't have a food processor, finely chop the dates and apricots, then mix in with everything else.

Roll the mixture into small balls with wet hands then roll them in a little extra desiccated coconut. I store mine in the fridge which makes them nice and chewy, but I don't think they need to be refrigerated.

This quantity of ingredients made thirteen decent-sized bliss balls. I may make half the quantity next time, simply because I have a mini food processor and I had to do the dried fruit in batches.

I used coconut oil because I already had a jar, however I've only ever put it on my face before, not put it in my food! I know coconut oil has excellent health-giving qualities, so I'm happy to have found a way to eat it. But of course, you could use another type of oil such as cold-pressed olive oil or any other oil that you have in your pantry.

I love peanut butter in my bliss balls but if you aren't a fan, just leave it out. And I'm definitely using cocoa powder in my next batch because chocolate-flavoured sounds good too!

Bonus Chapter.
Words to soothe your mind

When I first started writing this book, I noted down a list of words that I wanted the book to 'feel' like. I then went to an online thesaurus and searched for related words to bolster my stockpile.

It was actually a fun exercise, and in a short time I had compiled the most glorious list of words known to mankind (and put them in alphabetical order – luckily that's a quick and easy thing to do on the computer). Words which could soothe like a physical touch. (And whenever I got stuck for a word, I'd refer to my list!)

Would you like to wrap my list of words around you like a big fuzzy blanket too? Let's go:

Abundance

Alignment
Bliss
Brighten
Calm
Calming
Calmness
Charming
Cheer
Cheerful
Cheery
Clean
Collected
Comfort
Composed
Composure
Contentment
Cozy
Cultivated
Delight
Disciplined
Ease
Easy-going
Enchantment
Energizing
Enlighten
Enliven
Gentle
Good spirits
Happiness
Harmonious
Hearten

Heartening
Hospitality
Hygge
In harmony
Inspire
Joyful
Joyous
Kindness
Light-hearted
Neat as a button
Neaten
Order
Orderliness
Orderly
Peace
Peaceful
Pleasing
Pleasure
Quiet
Quietness
Quietude
Reassure
Reassuring
Refresh your spirit
Relaxation
Rest
Restful
Self-care
Serene
Serenity
Simplified

Sincerity
Smooth transition
Snug
Softness
Soothe
Soothing
Spa-like
Sparkling
Stillness
Strengthen
Tidy
Tranquil
Uncluttered
Vivacity
Warming
Warmth
Wellbeing

They are all so lovely! Do you feel as heartened and serene when you read through this list as I do? I really do think that words have a feeling associated with them, and not just from the meaning of the word, although that is a lot of it, of course.

Take tranquil for example. We know that it means to be still and peaceful, and a dictionary online says 'free from disturbance; calm' which is *so nice*. But the word 'tranquil' also has a watery, dreamy quality to it. Just saying it to myself as a settling mantra gives me that floaty, peaceful feeling. It's wonderful.

I don't really write poetry (and it's not what I'd go out searching for to read), but I had some fun writing out my own pieces. I'd almost go so far as to say they are paintings, but with words, rather than a picture done with water colour or oil paint.

I'd love to share these 'paintings' with you. They don't have names; they are just little pieces of a feeling.

~~

No. 1

Green
Soundless
Spiritual
Mossy
Serene
Sacred space
Silence
Earth
Stillness
Repose

~~

No. 2

Cooling
White light

Ethereal
Calm
Enlightened
Weightless
Feathery
Silver grey
Heavenly
Floating
Whispering

~~

No. 3

Romance
Love
Rosy pink
Heart-warming
Two
Glow
Welcoming
Bright
Golden

~~

No. 4

Wordsmith
Scholarly
Bookbinder

Claret leather
Writing
Tobacco
Open fire
Mohair rug

~~

No. 5

Breezy
Carefree
Ozone spray

~~

No. 6

Low light
Rumbling
Shades of grey
Daytime dark
Still
Cool
Dampness

~~

These pieces are the sum total of my poetry career, but I really treasure them. They encapsulate feelings, and I can immerse myself in those feelings at any time.

I'm sure words must activate different emotions in your body. I've never gone looking for proof via scientific texts, I just know for myself how good it feels to read a gentle and soothing book versus one that is more masculine, vicious, terrifying or jarring.

There is a place for all words though; it is invigorating to read a psychological thriller, however a feelgood chick lit book or calming work of non-fiction is more my cup of tea.

That's why I love reading books which settle the mind. They put me in a good place and I can face the world from there.

Some favourite calming books on my shelf are:

- 'The Gurus' Guide to Serenity' by Laurel and Sharon House (as already mentioned in Chapter 8 – 'Creating a spa atmosphere at home')

- 'Simple Abundance' by Sarah Ban Breathnach

- 'The Cozy Life' by Pia Edberg

- 'Living a Beautiful Life' by Alexandra Stoddard

- 'The Power' by Rhonda Byrne

- 'The Complete Idiot's Guide to Short Meditations' by Susan Gregg (despite the terrible title, it's a wonderful book)

I can read a few pages for a brief pause in my day, even just standing by my bookshelf, and when I pass that shelf, they greet me like friends. I love my books!

How you talk to yourself

The power of words extends not just to the words you take in, but also to the words you say to yourself: the exact same principle applies, whether it is out loud or in your head. It is so easy to see when others are being mean to themselves, or to someone else, but much harder to catch it when we are harsh on ourselves.

When our little rescue dogs get a fright or I yell at them to, 'Come here!' they'll run away from me. But if I call them over in a reassuring tone, they will happily come towards me and away from the danger on the road that I was yelling to them about.

It's the same with us. We can't criticize ourselves all day long and expect to be a happy and productive person. I started making progress with my health goals when I decided to stop telling myself that I was fat, lazy and had no willpower.

It makes so much sense when you see it written down, but when you are going through a normal day and feel hungry between meals so go and get a bag of potato chips out of the pantry, the ranting starts. 'You think these are good for you, Fiona? That they are going to help you look good this summer?' And so on.

But if I say to myself, "You're okay, let's wait until dinner time, it's not far away", or if I have eaten them, "That's okay, we've eaten them now, and they were good! But that was the last packet so let's just say no at the supermarket, yeah? It's much easier to say no then, than when they are in the kitchen."

It feels far more loving, and I happily go on with my day. Even if I ate those potato chips every single day, being mean to myself isn't going to change that. But being nice can. It drops the resistance and rebellion.

Your peaceful life tips:

- **Consider what reading material you are consuming**, especially at bed-time. If you love psychological thrillers, for example, like I do from time to time, keep them for during the day. I love to read a book before I fall to sleep, but the one time I read a particularly electrifying end to a thriller, it took a lot to calm me down enough to nod off!

- In your happylist notebook (from Chapter 3 – 'The magic of happylists'), **write down words which make you feel happy**, uplifted, alive, serene and calm. Add to them when you come across new words, and let them guide your decisions. For example: I love the word *serenity*. When I am thinking of what to browse on my iPad for a bit of downtime, I am guided by my serene wish to choose a lovely Kindle book, pretty Pinterest boards or inspiring Instagram accounts over the Daily Mail or gossipy Twitter threads. It is just as much fun and I feel so much better about myself afterwards.

- **Talk to yourself in a loving way**! Say it audibly if you want to. Sometimes I'll give myself a gentle kick if I've been wallowing, saying, 'Come on Fiona, let's go do something different.' And 'we' do. Try it for yourself!

21 ways to feel calm, soothed, relaxed and at peace, no matter what is happening around you

If you have read any of my other books, you will know that I love to finish off with an inspiring list, so please allow me to share my soothing tips to add to your peaceful life. Enjoy!

1. **Appreciate everything**. Keeping your *joie de vivre* is much easier when you take notice of the small pleasures around you. Taking enjoyment in everyday life is the secret to happiness perhaps, even more so than the 'big' things. Well, both are good, but make sure to appreciate the little things as well; there are certainly more of them!

2. **Make time for things that make you feel happy**. There are tons of little activities you can

do which will increase your happiness level. Many of them are free and don't take much time or energy. Stockpile your own list to choose from, and until you build up that stash, here are a few examples of my own:

- Yoga classes
- Walking outside
- Carrying out your household chores with plenty of time to spare so you are not rushed and can enjoy doing them
- Going to see a movie by yourself
- Reading at any time of the day
- A home spa day or evening
- Pottering – some call it 'puttering'
- Quiet time to yourself
- Sewing, knitting, needlework, patchwork, crochet – whatever craft you enjoy
- Window shopping and seeing what is new without spending a cent, except perhaps for a cold drink or coffee
- Early nights
- Planning ahead and being organized
- A tidy, clean, orderly, peaceful home
- Having a pet

Make your own list and do these things more.

3. **Tend to your life**. Tidy up loose ends, stop procrastinating (even if just for one day), do

things you have been putting off, get your admin up to date, throw out ten pieces of clutter, reconcile your bank accounts, clear off the kitchen counter or dining table and wipe it clean. Finish little jobs off, sort the mending pile once and for all, iron as you wash, get rid of things as you come across them – don't wait for a big clean-up day. Find the things that are stealing your peace and deal with them. Pick one thing and do it today!

4. **Plant flowers not weeds**. Try to keep your energy level positive by not dwelling on unpleasant or sad things if you can't do anything about them. Our mind is like a garden – if we don't plant flowers (good thoughts), then the weeds will take over (negative thoughts). If a weed pops up, replace it with a flower to crowd out that weed. As time goes on the flowers will regenerate naturally because positive thinking is just as much a habit as negative thinking.

5. **Re-read your favourite books**. Keep those titles together on your bookshelf or in a Kindle folder. Even browsing the titles will soothe you. In my collection are spiritually uplifting books from Rhonda Byrne, 'chick lit' by authors such as Sophie Kinsella and Jane Green (I love 'Jemima J'), my French Chic library with authors such as Anne Barone and Jennifer L. Scott, and many more. There doesn't need to be

a specific genre or type, just that the book brings about a peaceful and joyous sense of wellbeing in you.

6.   Take five minutes to **put an area in order**. Do it slowly and deliberately. Don't take on a huge job. Choose one little bothersome hotspot that can be made better in five minutes.

7.   **Soften what you listen to**. I have found beautiful music which now provides a serene background to my day, whether I'm driving or at home. Search on Spotify, YouTube or Apple Music for Windham Hill, Hilary Stagg, Peder B. Helland and Kevin Kern. You can also search for mixes such as 'relaxing study music' or 'coffeehouse relaxing jazz'. My current favourite is a great YouTube channel called 'Café Music BGM Channel' with lots of different tracks. It is soft background music which is uplifting and upbeat: perfect!

8.   **Find your feeling**. Ask yourself what you need to feel good on an everyday basis and how can you make it the easiest to obtain. For me, it's a feeling of peace. If I felt peaceful every day, no matter how much I had on, I'd be golden. That then leads me to the question to ask myself regularly: 'How can I feel peaceful today?' What about you? Is it peace? Radiance? Happiness? Hope?

9. **Declutter by numbers**. This little technique has been so fun and helpful to me. You can borrow my numbers, or someone else's, or choose your own. It's a really simple trick! Simply ask yourself, 'What five things can I declutter from these everyday dishes?' or 'What are three things in my closet right now that I can't wait to donate?'

   Or you could choose to declutter ten items a day – each day put ten things into your donation box. Actually rove around the house looking! It's amazing, when I think in terms of numbers, whether it's a category or in general, it makes the process of letting go far easier.

10. **Make inner peace your highest goal**. Getting worked up over little things makes you feel awful and it's not good for you, both mentally and physically. Take on board to 'make inner peace your highest goal', and you will find situations that you would have become quite annoyed with are simply smoothed over. Instead of becoming peeved over a minor annoyance, make inner peace your highest goal and feel instantly transformed.

11. **Be organized**. When an item has an easily accessible place to live it will more likely get put away. Clutter builds up when something has nowhere permanent to go. It's been said that the

more in control of your life you are the happier you feel, and I agree with that.

Something small you can do is to find homes for all your possessions by decluttering and organizing your living space. When you take control of your home and make it your oasis of calm away from the outside world (which is largely out of our control), you are taking control of your life.

12. **Seek beauty**. Large-format glossy home-and-garden picture books are wonderful to flip through with a cup of tea in the afternoon. It is fifteen minutes of relaxation and you will feel rich afterwards.

    Visiting a beautiful wine store or curated homeware store gives the same feeling. You are physically in another world and you soak it up. Sometimes you might buy something and sometimes not. You don't need to take anything physical home with you to be able to absorb that feeling of elevated wellbeing and elegance.

13. **Be nice to yourself**. Filter everything you say in your mind through the question, 'Would I speak to a dear friend like this?' If the answer is 'no', try changing your thoughts to something you would say as a kind and supportive friend. Even though this may feel a bit fake to start with

you'll soon get used to it, and over time it will even begin to give you a warm, loved feeling.

14. **Simplify, simplify, simplify**. It's the key to a peaceful life! The more you declutter, the happier you are with the things you already own. The more you streamline your schedule and eliminate things that drain you energetically, the lighter you will feel. Always be looking for ways in which you can make your life less complicated.

15. **A peaceful sleep**. When you are in bed waiting to go to sleep at night, imagine yourself floating inside a bubble. You are surrounded by soft, iridescent light and you feel so relaxed. Just float there in that bubble and soak in the feeling of love, wonder, and peace as you drift off to sleep.

16. **Change how you feel**. Small things can make a huge difference: take deep breaths, breathing right down into your stomach. Relax all the muscles in your body with a still, calm mind. Go through all your muscles one-by-one with your eyes closed for a minute, and relax them.

17. **Collect inspiring questions**. I have a place where I note down journal prompts and questions to use. There are so many good ones and I'm always finding more! Spending fifteen

minutes answering a good question in my notebook always leaves me feeling happier and more inspired. Start your own collection off with these:

- How can I feel proud of myself today?
- How can I make this (idea/project/goal) easier and more fun?
- How will my life be different when I (insert dream or goal here)? (Buy a house, lose weight, etc)
- What is one thing I can say 'no' to that will bring me more peace?
- How can I give love to my body today?
- What are all the good things that have happened this week?
- How can I make my life simpler?

18. **Take care of all that you have, exquisitely**. Appreciate your home and everything around you. Re-commit to living where you love by loving where you live. Bloom where you are planted, even if you want more in the future. And until that time, figure out how you want to feel in your home. If it's happy, carefree, content and peaceful, *make the decision* to feel happy, carefree, content and peaceful and focus on things that make you *feel* happy, carefree, content and peaceful.

19. **Past-Present-Future**. If you're feeling 'sped up' with the thoughts in your head, come back to the present. Dream up goals, ideas and plans for the future but don't go too far forward. Feel nostalgia for the good times in the past, funny family stories and favourite memories, but don't live there.

    Reserve most of yourself for the present; both in your attention, and also what you have in your home and how you keep your home. Take inspiration from the past, and excitement for the future and make today your everything. Today is where it's at. How can you make today the best day ever?

20. **Dream up your most feminine life**, right down to the tiny details, and surround yourself in a froth of ladylike delights – even if most of them are in your mind. I love the Ralph Lauren home aesthetic, sort of an English country house style, but it isn't particularly girly. However, I have pockets of indulgence such as our bedroom décor, and I spend time every day moisturizing my skin, putting on a little bit of makeup, doing my hair etc. And I like to keep a feminine state of mind too, with how I think, speak, act, walk and hold myself. I truly think as women that we blossom with touches of beauty and femininity in our daily life.

21. **Fill your life with beauty, creativity and pleasure**. No matter how much we have going on in our lives, no matter how busy our days are, and no matter how much money we have, we owe it to ourselves to bring beauty, creativity and pleasure into our daily life. It's what we are here for. The human being was designed to seek pleasure, have desires and be creative.

Creative in the way women have babies, cook meals, and adorn our home. Creative in art, writing, flower arranging, writing, sewing, crafting and gardening. You may personally find creativity in 'traditionally male' pursuits (my sister loves doing all kinds of woodwork!) It doesn't matter. What matters is that you have a creative expression. Beauty, creativity and pleasure run alongside each other. You create something and it brings beauty to your life, giving pleasure at the same time.

A note from the author

Thank you for reading 'The Peaceful Life'! My sincere wish is that you have finished this book in a refreshed, grounded, and inspired state of mind; that you feel brand new and hopeful.

Each of us has a lot going on in our lives. We are zipping in different directions many times a day. For this reason, it is imperative that we slow down, even if only in our minds, and reduce stress as much as possible in order to be our healthiest and happiest selves.

It can be done with intention and focus, even in scary times. We have the power to direct our mind and we can live in serenity amongst chaos, truly! Ask yourself on a regular basis, 'How can I reduce the stress in my day?' and 'How can I make my life more peaceful?' Enjoy the little (and big) things in your wondrous existence.

Don't feel that your life is ordinary, mundane or dull. You can choose wonder, symphony and fireworks if you want to, even while doing exactly the same things as before, working the same hours and being around the same people.

But as you heighten your thoughts, so your actions will follow, and before long, you will find yourself doing different, better things. Follow the breadcrumbs of your happiness and go forth with love, serenity and joy. I will see you there!

If you enjoyed this book, I would be so grateful for a review on Amazon, even if it's only a few words. Reviews are very important to authors! It's how other readers find our books. I read all reviews of my books to get your feedback, and hope to make my future books better by doing this.

Thank you in advance if you are happy to leave a review, and I wish you a beautiful and peaceful day in the gloriousness that is your life.

See you soon, and all my best to you!

Fiona

About the author

Fiona Ferris is passionate about and has studied the topic of living well for more than twenty years, in particular that a simple and beautiful life can be achieved without spending a lot of money.

Fiona finds inspiration from all over the place including Paris and France, the countryside, big cities, fancy hotels, music, beautiful scents, magazines, books, all those fabulous blogs out there, people, pets, nature, other countries and cultures; really, everywhere she looks.

Fiona lives in the beautiful and sunny wine region of Hawke's Bay, New Zealand, with her husband, Paul, their rescue cats Jessica and Nina and rescue dogs Daphne and Chloe.

To learn more about Fiona, you can connect with her at:

howtobechic.com
fionaferris.com
facebook.com/fionaferrisauthor
twitter.com/fiona_ferris
instagram.com/fionaferrisnz
youtube.com/fionaferris

Book Bonuses

http://bit.ly/ThirtyChicDaysBookBonuses

Type in the link above to receive your free special bonuses.

'21 ways to be chic' is a fun list of chic living reminders, with an MP3 recording to accompany it so you can listen on the go as well.

Excerpts from Fiona's books in PDF format.

You will also **receive a subscription** to Fiona's blog *'How to be Chic'*, for inspiration on living a simple, beautiful and successful life.